ENCORE! 3 TENORS

CollinsPublishersSanFrancisco

A Division of HarperCollins*Publishers*

Good evening, ladies and gentlemen, and welcome to Encore! The Three Tenors. There isn't a producer in the world who wouldn't cherish the opportunity to be able to present this extraordinary gathering of talent. Nor is there a country on the planet that wouldn't want to be the host of such an important event. I am very proud to have been given that great honor, and prouder still that the concert is happening in Los Angeles, the world's entertainment capital.

We can reflect on tonight's brilliant performance knowing that we are privileged participants in one of the landmark events marking the close of the twentieth century. And it is marvelous that well over a billion more music lovers will be able to enjoy the concert later through television and recordings.

The excitement around this evening's concert has been building for months. More than fifty thousand tickets were sold long in advance of the event, most of them to an audience that has never been inside an opera house, but which loves these artists through their recordings and television appearances. If only a handful of this audience will be inspired to visit an opera house for the first time because of tonight's performance, then these maestros are furthering my dream to extend opera to the general public.

I cannot give enough thanks to the hundreds of artists and technical experts, as well as to the hundreds of other coworkers—and most importantly, to the staff of the Rudas Organization, whose two years of preparation have made this concert possible.

I would like to extend my deepest gratitude to Mr. Ahmet Ertegun and Mr. Alan Rothenberg of World Cup USA 1994 for selecting this performance as the "Final Concert" of the world's greatest sporting event. And my gratitude also extends to Mr. Peter O'Malley, President of the Los Angeles Dodgers, for having the foresight to know that this beautiful stadium would be naturally suited for the transformation into a spectacular "Concert Hall". They and their magnificent staffs have made the dream a reality.

It gives me great pleasure to share with you the gifts of these extraordinary artists, performers not just for our time, but forever.

Enjoy the performance!

Tibor Rudas

The Very Last Note of the Rome Concert, 1990.

On July 16, 1994, the moon shines down on Los Angeles to reveal an astounding sight: Dodger Stadium is transformed from ballpark to concert hall, where some of the most gifted artists of our time gather to enthrall an audience. The conjunction of these stellar performers in concert creates a kind of spontaneous combustion, a brilliant explosion radiating an excitement rarely seen in the world of classical music. And they come together not only as colleagues but also as friends—and friendly competitors.

Music is not the only tie that binds them. They are all passionate fans of the single most popular sport in the world—soccer. As José Carreras puts it, "It's not just a sport but a social phenomenon!" It was the World Cup Finals in 1990 that drew them together for the first time in Rome. They then waited for four years to repeat their collaboration, rejecting almost daily offers to perform together. For Plácido Domingo, "The event could have taken place anywhere, but the best place was Dodger Stadium…" to sing in celebration of their lifelong love affair with soccer.

The singers root for the teams of their home countries—Spain for Carreras and Domingo and Italy for Pavarotti. "We do it for the Cup," says Luciano Pavarotti, emphasizing their collective affection for the game. When asked which of the teams he supports, the ever diplomatic Bombay-born Zubin Mehta responds, "In my country, we play cricket! My main concern is that if Spain and Italy are playing against each other in the final match the day after the concert,

4

my conducting job will be that much harder!"

To make this concert possible, the four principal artists are surrounded and supported by a huge team of nearly 1,000 musicians, performers, artisans, craftsmen, technicians, engineers, and other staff. Enthusiastic fans in more than 100 countries will be able to witness this concert on television and listen to it on radio simulcasts. Fourteen video cameras, under the supervision of director Bill Cosel, are needed to capture the vast scope of the action. Later, a documentary supervised by David Dinkins, Jr., will share the behind-the-scenes activity of the past year. And within one month of this extraordinary concert, a live album will be released in the United States by Atlantic Records and internationally by Teldec Classics.

With the global audience in mind, the four principal artists have conceived the concert program with care. The arias and songs to be performed are among the most beautiful ever composed and are the favorites of fans everywhere. They are the songs that inspire us, brighten our spirits, and move our hearts.

The superb quality of the concert's sound is the result of a computer-designed system which provides acoustical enhancement of the voices and orchestra. Specifically developed for this occasion, its sophisticated design enables audience members to enjoy the performance just as if they were in the concert hall or opera house.

Unlike a public-address system, which projects the sound into the far reaches of the stadium simply by making the music louder, this special equipment takes the acoustical properties of the arena into account and reinforces the sound where it is needed. Dodger Stadium is ideal for this event because of its unique shape: the area behind the stage is open, allowing the sound a natural means of escape rather than containing it only to reverberate unpleasantly within.

Sound Designer Alexander Yuill-Thornton II and engineering specialists Jimmy Lock and John Pellowe have been studying the stadium's acoustics for the past year, calibrating the

equipment to provide just the right level of support for the voices and orchestra. This system guarantees without a doubt the finest concert sound ever experienced out-of-doors. The painstaking care being given to the stadium sound will also make it possible to create an outstanding audio recording of the concert for later release on CD and audio cassette.

To take the best advantage of Dodger Stadium's architecture, Tibor Rudas conceived of a plan to place the stage between the embracing arms of the grandstand pavilions, transforming the baseball

stadium into an amphitheater. The result of his planning is an elegant setting recalling the architectural grandeur of classical antiquity.

Craftsmen from three continents have collaborated on the massive project. The stage roof, podium, and risers were designed and built in Australia. The twenty massive columns designed by László Székely were constructed in Hungary. The overall scenic design has been created by American art director Rene Lagler.

Lighting the setting has been the biggest technical challenge, since there can be no lighting towers blocking the audience's view. Lighting Designer Olin Younger has conquered this problem with the innovative use of state-of-the-art equipment.

The rear and sides of the stage are open, revealing a verdant backdrop and two towering water cascades. The "forest" is not only decorative but also functions as an acoustic shell. The field is covered with a four-level seating area similar to that found in concert halls but never before attempted in a sports venue, providing the audience with unobstructed views.

PERFORMERS

ENCORE! 3 TENORS

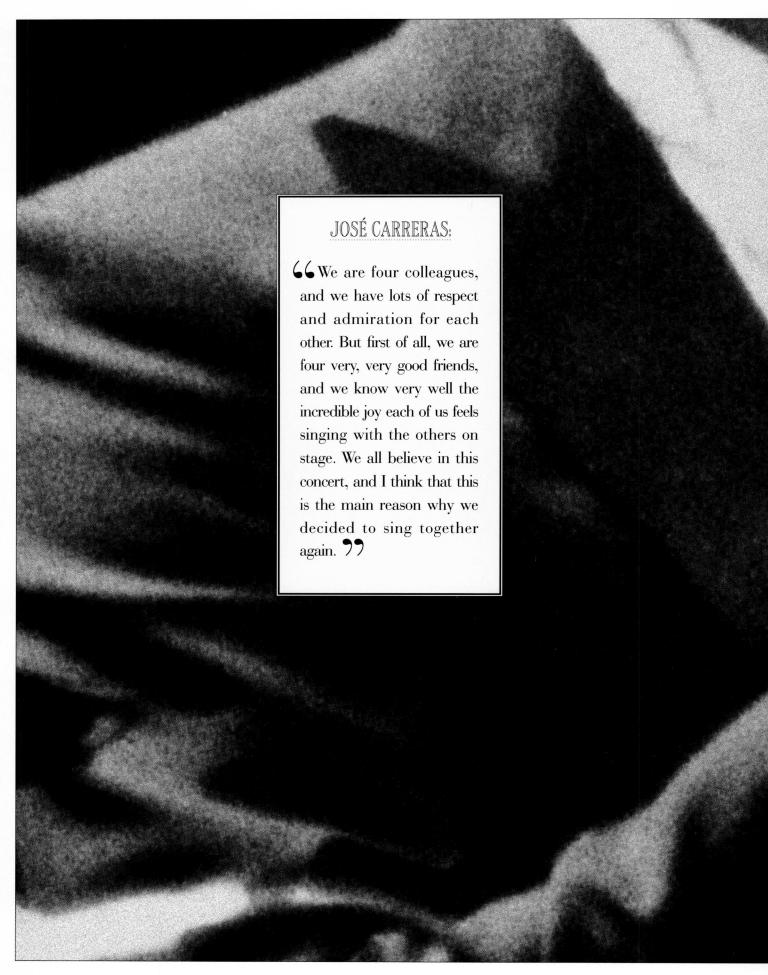

JOSÉ CARRERAS:

"We are four colleagues, and we have lots of respect and admiration for each other. But first of all, we are four very, very good friends, and we know very well the incredible joy each of us feels singing with the others on stage. We all believe in this concert, and I think that this is the main reason why we decided to sing together again."

JOSÉ CARRERAS holds a singular place among today's most celebrated tenors. Acclaimed for the rich, natural lyricism of his voice and an arresting intensity of delivery, Mr. Carreras has brought a distinctive sensibility to the opera stage.

He was born on December 5, 1947, in the Spanish region of Catalonia, known for its proud and individualistic people. An irrepressible performer as a boy, his natural vocal gifts were apparent from an early age as he sang along with the recordings of Mario Lanza and Giuseppe di Stefano. At age eleven, on the stage of the famed Gran Teatro del Liceo in Barcelona under the baton of José Iturbi, he made his operatic debut as the narrator in de Falla's *Master Peter's Puppet Show*.

Although certain his career would be on the opera stage, he pursued a more practical curriculum at the University of Barcelona, studying chemistry and intending to join in the family cosmetics concern. Still, the voice lessons continued, and his fate was sealed in 1971 when he won the International Verdi Singing Competition in Parma, Italy. The prize included an engagement as Rodolfo in *La Bohème*; a performance that prompted rapturous ovations from the demanding Teatro Regio audience.

He made his international debut in a concert

performance of Donizetti's *Maria Stuarda* at Festival Hall, London, in 1971. Successes in important roles at opera houses around the world soon broadened his reputation. He sang his first Pinkerton in *Madama Butterfly* with the New York City Opera in 1972; his Metropolitan Opera debut as Cavaradossi in *Tosca* came in 1974, the same year he triumphed at London's Covent Garden, Vienna's Staatsoper, and Milan's La Scala in *Un Ballo in Maschera*. By 1975, he had conquered all of the world's leading stages.

Herbert von Karajan invited Mr. Carreras to sing in Verdi's *Requiem* during the 1976 Salzburg Easter Festival. Performances and recordings of various works followed, during which the maestro and the tenor cultivated an intense artistic collaboration and close friendship that was to last the next twelve years.

Recent triumphs include *Fedora* at La Scala and Verdi's *Stiffelio* at Covent Garden, a universally acclaimed performance for which he was awarded the 1992/93 Sir Lawrence Olivier Award. He also served as Musical

CARR

Director for the opening and closing ceremonies of the 1992 Summer Olympic Games in his beloved native Barcelona.

Over the course of his career, Mr. Carreras has made a prodigious number of recordings, including more than 50 complete operas and 40 classical and popular recitals. He has forayed into lighter repertoire, encompassing Spanish and Italian songs, works by Andrew Lloyd Webber, Rodgers and Hammerstein's *South Pacific*, the multiple-award-winning recording *West Side Story*, conducted by its composer Leonard Bernstein, and a tribute to his early vocal inspiration, Mario Lanza. Several of these recordings have achieved gold and platinum status. Many video recordings of his performances in leading roles are also available. His video portrait, *A Life Story*, won the International Emmy Award. He has also made a motion picture,

Romanza Final, in which he portrays the life of tenor Julian Gayarre.

Public awareness of his struggle against a near fatal encounter with leukemia in 1987 inspired millions with his courage.

In 1988, The José Carreras International Leukemia Foundation was established in Barcelona. With the collaboration of a highly qualified worldwide team, including Professor E. D. Thomas, the winner of the 1990 Nobel Prize for Medicine, Mr. Carreras successfully governs his organization as its president. His autobiography, *José Carreras, Singing From the Soul*, tells the extraordinary story of his life and career, his illness, and his devotion to his family and children.

José Carreras is a hero for our time, a sensitive artist and courageous humanitarian who has enriched the world with his considerable gifts.

66 We had a lot of ideas about what to sing in this concert. There is a vast repertoire, not only in opera but also in the different songs that we sing—the crossovers, the Neapolitan songs—the legacy we received from singers like Caruso, Schipa, Gigli, Lanza, and di Stefano. So believe me, the repertoire has always been the easiest part of planning this concert. 99

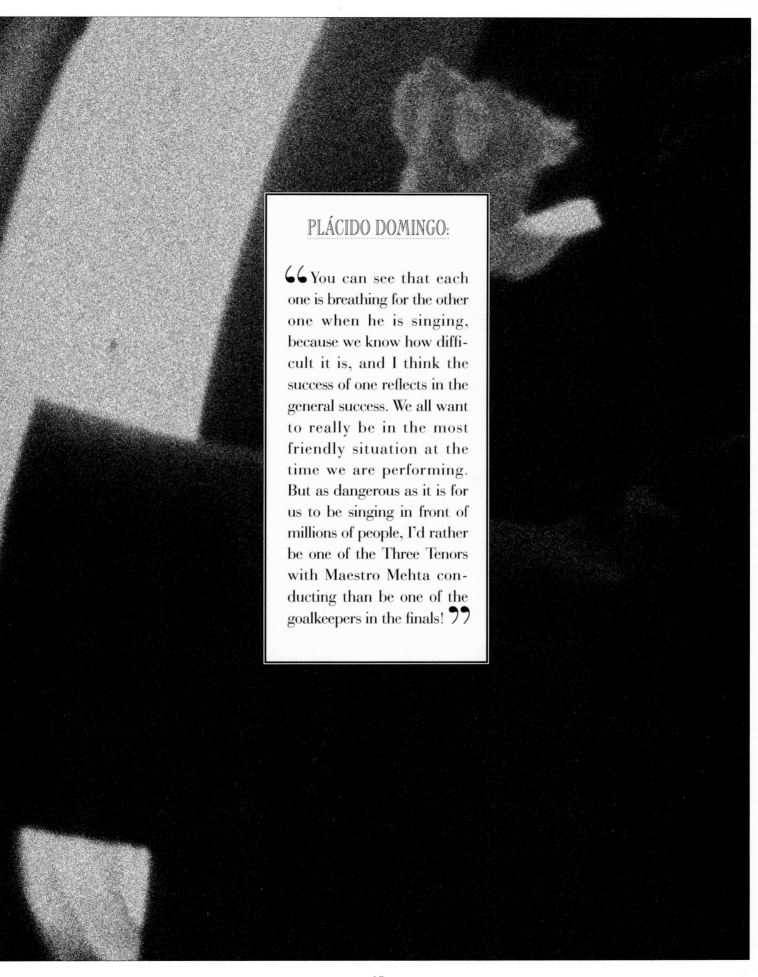

PLÁCIDO DOMINGO:

66 You can see that each one is breathing for the other one when he is singing, because we know how difficult it is, and I think the success of one reflects in the general success. We all want to really be in the most friendly situation at the time we are performing. But as dangerous as it is for us to be singing in front of millions of people, I'd rather be one of the Three Tenors with Maestro Mehta conducting than be one of the goalkeepers in the finals! 99

PLÁCIDO DOMINGO stands at the pinnacle of a career that spans virtually every role in the tenor repertoire and is honored and celebrated by millions of admiring fans around the world. He is a peerless singing actor whose burnished voice is instantly recognizable and renowned for its power, depth, and subtlety.

He was born in Madrid on January 21, 1941. His parents, popular zarzuela performers, formed their own company and moved the family to Mexico City when he was eight; his early musical education included experiences performing in their productions. As a student he enjoyed soccer, playing goalkeeper on his school team. Among his classmates, three became professional players, including World Cup player José Luis González.

Plácido Domingo began his career singing in his parents' zarzuelas, and he even had a part in the Mexican première of *My Fair Lady*. In 1959, after a successful audition with the Mexican National Opera, he began to master the operatic repertory and debuted in *La Traviata* in Monterrey in 1961.

The Israel National Opera offered him a six-month engagement in 1962; there he thrived during the next two and a half years, singing 280 performances in 12 leading roles.

Successful performances in the United States in 1965 preceded his New York City Opera debut in *Madama Butterfly* on October 17. He made his debut at the Metropolitan Opera on September 28, 1968, in *Adriana Lecouvreur*. In the twenty-five years since, he has sung more performances at the Met than in any other opera house in the world and more opening nights at the Met than anyone since Caruso. He and Luciano Pavarotti recently celebrated their 25th anniversaries there together with a glittering Opening Night Gala.

Plácido Domingo regularly performs in the world's leading opera houses, singing a truly amazing number of Italian and French roles. His ever-expanding foray into the repertoire has resulted in the recordings of a number of German roles: *Meistersinger, Lohengrin, Tannhäuser, the Flying Dutchman*, and the Emperor in *Die Frau ohne Schatten*. Onstage performances of German roles include *Lohengrin, Parsifal*, Siegmund in *Die Walküre*, and an upcoming performance as Tristan in 1996. He constantly challenges himself by learning new roles and champions new works, performing in such varied compositions as

Don Rodrigo by Alberto Ginastera, which inaugurated the New York State Theatre at Lincoln Center in 1966, and *Goya*, written for him by Gian Carlo Menotti, which had its world première in Washington, D.C., in 1986.

He is a prolific recording artist, so far releasing 87 complete performances of 59 different operas and numerous solo and duet discs, eight of which have received Grammy Awards. He is as much at home with the popular repertoire as with the classics. *Perhaps Love*, recorded with John Denver, sold several million copies worldwide, and other successful crossover albums followed. He is often seen in televised performances and has starred in three acclaimed opera films: Zeffirelli's *La Traviata* and *Otello* and Rosi's *Carmen*. In July of 1992, he portrayed Cavaradossi in an Emmy-winning production of *Tosca*, broadcast live from its three historic Roman locations.

Although "Plácido Domingo" might translate from Spanish into English as "peaceful Sunday," his life is anything but. He has simultaneously pursued a successful conducting career nearly as long as his operatic one, leading performances in major opera houses and concert halls since making his conducting debut with *La Traviata* at the New York City Opera during its 1973–74 season. He employs his considerable managerial skills as Artistic Consultant to the Los Angeles Music Center Opera and was Music Director for the 1992 Seville World's Fair. Closer to the heart, his tireless philanthropic efforts on

behalf of the 1985 Mexican earthquake victims have raised millions of dollars.

Whether thrilling an opera house audience with his voice, inspiring an orchestra from the podium, or employing his expertise to bring new productions to the stage, Plácido Domingo is a renaissance man in the truest sense of the word.

INGO

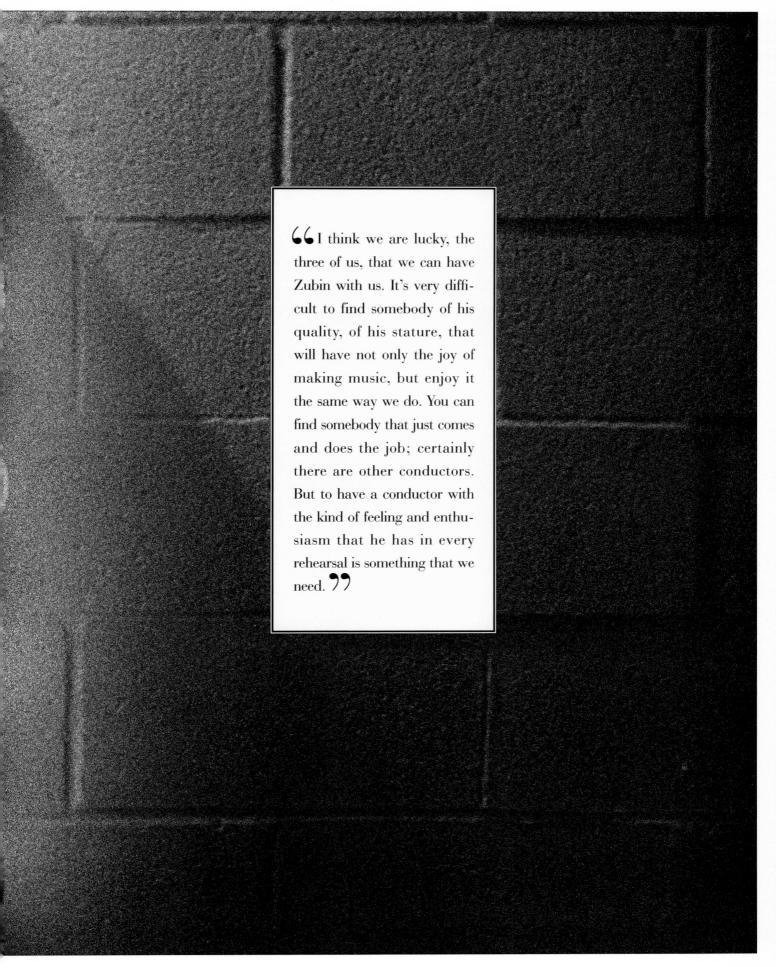

"I think we are lucky, the three of us, that we can have Zubin with us. It's very difficult to find somebody of his quality, of his stature, that will have not only the joy of making music, but enjoy it the same way we do. You can find somebody that just comes and does the job; certainly there are other conductors. But to have a conductor with the kind of feeling and enthusiasm that he has in every rehearsal is something that we need. "

LUCIANO PAVAROTTI:

66 When I am singing—in that precise moment, not before, not after, but in that precise moment—I sing for the composer because it's the only way to do a good interpretation. If you could see my face immediately after the song is finished, you would see my concentration, and then I smile because I become myself again. But at this precise moment I sing for *one* person—not one million. 99

LUCIANO PAVAROTTI makes an immense impact on the world of classical music, broadening its horizons and attracting countless fans. Thanks to his thrilling voice and unique personality, the name "Pavarotti" has become a household word, synonymous with the highest standards of performance.

He was born in Modena, Italy, on October 12, 1935, the first child and only son of a baker. As a boy, sports occupied much of his time. In fact, he earned his first local fame as a member of the town's soccer team, excelling at the game he has followed passionately ever since. He first sang in the Modena chorus with his father, a fervent lover of opera and gifted amateur tenor. When the chorus won first prize in an international competition, the youngster was hooked.

His debut came on April 29, 1961, as Rodolfo in *La Bohème*, at the opera house in Reggio Emilia. That success led to engagements throughout Italy and the world, where he conquered audiences in Amsterdam, Vienna, Zurich, and London. His American debut came in February, 1965, in a Miami production of *Lucia di Lammermoor* with Joan Sutherland, the beginning of what would become their historic partnership. Debuts in *La Bohème* at La Scala, San Francisco, and New York won the hearts of fans around the world.

But it wasn't until February 17, 1972, that the Pavarotti phenomenon was born, in a production of *La Fille du Régiment* at New York's Metropolitan Opera. Responding to Pavarotti's aria containing nine effortless high Cs, the audience erupted in a frenzied ovation, and the young tenor's reputation soared into the stratosphere.

Maestro Pavarotti appears on the greatest international opera and concert stages, collaborating with the world's most gifted conductors and singers, on television, in movies, and in arena concerts. His recordings, each and every one a best-seller, include collections of arias and recital programs, a live concert from Carnegie Hall, and anthologies of Neapolitan and other Italian songs.

PAVAI

His frequent television appearances in performance as well as in documentaries and on talk shows continue to add to his musical renown. His performance as Rodolfo thrilled America in the historic first *Live from the Met* telecast in March of 1977, which attracted one of the largest audiences ever for a televised opera. And from that same stage, he and Plácido Domingo together celebrated their 25th anniversaries with an Opening Night Gala performance in the fall of 1993.

He consistently draws record-breaking audiences to sold-out arena concerts in many countries and shares his music with huge audiences in the great public parks of the world. His televised concert in London's Hyde Park, in the presence of Charles and Diana, the Prince and Princess of Wales, was the first concert in the history of the park featuring classical music and drew a record attendance of some 150,000 people. In June 1993, more than 500,000 fans gathered to enjoy his performance on the Great Lawn of New York's Central Park, while millions more around the world watched on television.

The following September, singing in the shadow of the Eiffel Tower in Paris, he thrilled the hearts of an estimated 300,000 music lovers.

Maestro Pavarotti is also dedicated to the development of the careers of young singers. In 1982 he initiated an ongoing international vocal competition with the Opera Company of Philadelphia. He also conducts standing-room-only master classes at conservatories around the world.

He still makes his home in Modena, taking time each summer for a retreat to his vacation home in Pesaro, a converted farmhouse overlooking the Adriatic. There he relaxes with his wife, Adua, and their three daughters, other family members, and friends, preparing sumptuous meals with the region's excellent food and wine and riding his

horses in the surrounding countryside.

Illuminated by his radient personality and propelled by his zest for life Luciano Pavarotti's golden voice transcends the walls of the opera house to reach inside every human heart and mind.

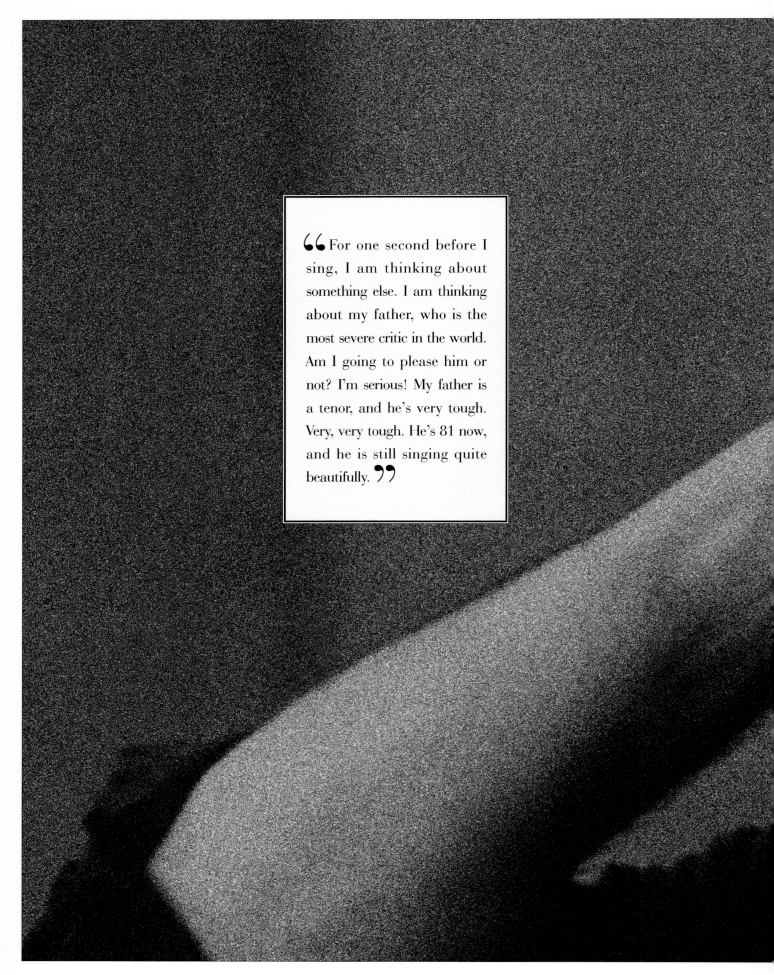

66 For one second before I sing, I am thinking about something else. I am thinking about my father, who is the most severe critic in the world. Am I going to please him or not? I'm serious! My father is a tenor, and he's very tough. Very, very tough. He's 81 now, and he is still singing quite beautifully. **99**

ZUBIN MEHTA:

66 The first time proved a concert like this might attract new audiences to opera, although it was never our intention that it would reach that many millions or billions of people. But the number of people that came closer to opera as a result of the Rome concert only gave us the impetus that this was again the right time to do one more. And we are absolutely sure that this time, especially in the United States, the impact will be of a very robust nature. 99

ZUBIN MEHTA has achieved a unique position among conductors in the world today. He was born in Bombay, India on April 29, 1936. His parents discouraged his early interest in becoming a classical musician, even though his father, Mehli Mehta, was a violinist and co-founder of the Bombay Symphony. Mr. Mehta was to study medicine; but by the age of eighteen, the die was cast when he had the chance to lead his father's orchestra in several performances. He soon abandoned his medical studies to pursue his musical destiny at the Academy of Music in Vienna.

Seven years later, at the remarkably young age of twenty-five, he had conducted both the Vienna and Berlin Philharmonics, and, from 1961 to 1967, acted as Music Director of the Montreal Symphony. In 1962, the Los Angeles Philharmonic appointed him Music Director, a

post he held for sixteen years; this concert is a happy reunion with that great orchestra. He accepted the appointment of Music Director with the New York Philharmonic in 1978, serving with them until 1991.

In 1961, a lifelong bond was begun when he first led the Israel Philharmonic Orchestra. He was appointed its Music Advisor in 1969, Music Director in 1977, and, in 1981, its Music Director for Life. Numerous concerts, recordings, and tours of all five continents have generated more than 1500 concerts with that orchestra.

During his thirteen year tenure with the New York Philharmonic, Maestro Mehta conducted more than 1000 concerts and held the post longer than any music director in the Orchestra's modern history. During his tenure, he conducted the Philharmonic on a number of major tours covering all five continents. The tour especially dear to his heart was to Asia in 1984, which culminated in his home town of Bombay. In June 1988 he led a ten-day visit to the Soviet Union that included an historic joint concert with the State Symphony Orchestra of the Soviet Ministry of Culture in Moscow's Gorky Park. In May 1991, the Maestro concluded his tenure with three performances celebrating the 100th anniversary of Carnegie Hall, followed by a series of performances

MEHT

of Schoenberg's *Gurrelieder*. In the fall of 1992, he returned to conduct the world premier of Olivier Messiaen's last symphony, "*Èclairs sur l'Au Delá*," and joined in the Philharmonic's 150th Anniversary Concert.

His love of opera has led to many productions, including Puccini's Tosca with Luciano Pavarotti at Covent Garden.His 1993 debut with the Lyric Opera of Chicago commenced a four-year commitment to conduct Wagner's "Ring" cycle. Since 1986, he has also acted as Music Advisor and Chief Conductor to the Maggio Musicale Fiorentino, a renowned summer festival in Florence. There, he recently completed a cycle of Mozart

operas, produced under the direction of Jonathan Miller.

Maestro Mehta is also known to audiences through his frequent appearances on *Live from Lincoln Center* and other television broadcasts. In July 1992, he joined forces with Plácido Domingo and Catherine Malfitano in an unprecedented live telecast of *Tosca*, performed at the locations and at the exact times of day specified in the score. The broadcast was seen in 107 countries and won him his second Emmy.

During the past twenty years, Mr. Mehta has done extensive concert, opera and recording work with tenors Carreras, Domingo and Pavarotti, including: an upcoming première of Verdi's *Jerusalem* with Mr. Carreras at the Vienna State Opera, Puccini's *Girl of the Golden West* and *Tosca* and Verdi's *Il Trovatore* with Mr. Domingo, and a legendary recording of *Turandot* with Mr. Pavarotti.

Today, Mr. Mehta continues his busy schedule leading major orchestras and opera companies the world over, including the London, Vienna and Berlin Philharmonics, the Vienna Staatsoper, and of course, the Israel Philharmonic Orchestra.

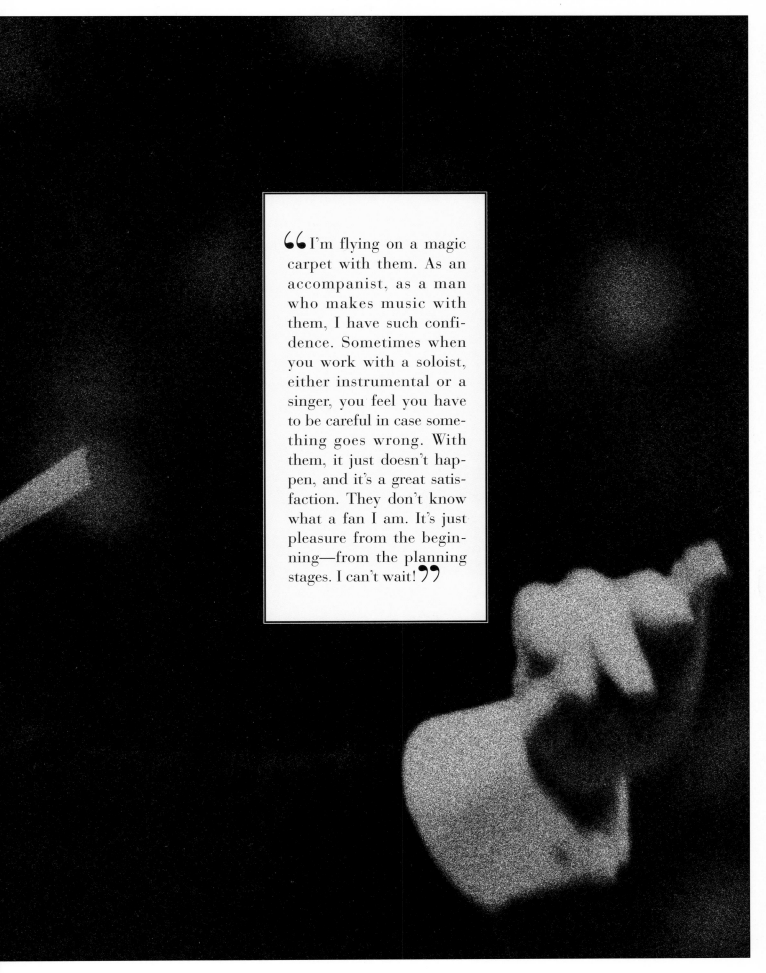

66 I'm flying on a magic carpet with them. As an accompanist, as a man who makes music with them, I have such confidence. Sometimes when you work with a soloist, either instrumental or a singer, you feel you have to be careful in case something goes wrong. With them, it just doesn't happen, and it's a great satisfaction. They don't know what a fan I am. It's just pleasure from the beginning—from the planning stages. I can't wait! **99**

For more than 75 years, the Los Angeles Philharmonic has brought pride to the citizens of Los Angeles with a diverse roster of musical performances that is enjoyed by more than one million concertgoers annually. The orchestra has developed steadily in artistic stature and prominence since its founding in 1919 and ranks among the world's leading international symphonic organizations. The brilliant Finnish conductor Esa-Pekka Salonen, about to begin his third season as Music Director, leads the Philharmonic toward the next century as it looks forward to the move into its new home in the Walt Disney Concert Hall in 1997. Nine other renowned conductors have led the orchestra since its founding, including the recent tenures of André Previn and Carlo Maria Giulini. This performance reunites the orchestra with another of its celebrated music directors, Zubin Mehta, who served the longest, from 1962 until 1978.

The orchestra has a commitment to share a broad range of the musical repertoire in order to satisfy the diverse tastes of its audience. Giving some 300 concerts, recitals, and special programs each season, it regularly performs an impressive variety of music, from the masterworks of Mozart, Beethoven, and Tchaikovsky to premières by important living composers. Its musicians participate in a variety of chamber music and contemporary music concerts, community activities, and educational programs for children and their parents. In addition to its winter season at the Dorothy Chandler Pavilion, the orchestra has made its summer home at the world famous Hollywood Bowl, since 1922, where it plays to huge and appreciative audiences each year. The orchestra has performed with Luciano Pavarotti at the Hollywood Bowl several times.

The Los Angeles Philharmonic has a distinguished touring history, playing in cities across the United States and around the world for nearly forty years. In August 1992, it became the first American orchestra in residence for both opera and concerts at the Salzburg Festival, winning international acclaim for its performances of Messiaen's monumental opera *Saint François d'Assise*, in a new production led by Maestro Salonen and directed by the orchestra's creative consultant, Peter Sellars. More recently, the orchestra was in residence at the Lucerne Easter Festival (1993), and in March of 1994 they toured Taiwan and Japan. Salonen and the Philharmonic will return to Europe later this summer, touring the major music festivals in August and September.

Los Angeles has traditionally been associated with tremors, not tenors. Indeed, until 1986, the city had the dubious distinction of being the last major population center in the United States without its own large-scale opera company. In its first eight seasons, however, the Los Angeles Music Center Opera—known informally as the L.A. Opera—has proven that the city provides as hospitable a climate for Verdi as it does for verdant lawns.

In 1984, after two decades of importing other companies to the Dorothy Chandler Pavilion, the Music Center Opera Association hired Peter Hemmings to be its first General Director, with the task of creating a company.

At the same time, Plácido Domingo became the company's Artistic Consultant, performing there regularly as both a singer and a conductor. The first season in 1986–87 consisted of 21 performances of five operas. For the 1994–95 season, the company will present 54 performances of eight operas.

Among the company's most noteworthy productions are Richard Strauss' *Salome*, directed by Sir Peter Hall and starring Maria Ewing; Wagner's *Tristan und Isolde*, conducted by Zubin Mehta and designed by world-renowned Los Angeles artist David Hockney; and Prokofiev's *The Fiery Angel*, directed by Andrei Serban and designed by Robert Israel.

In 1992, the company hosted the Finnish National Opera in its world première of Aulis Sallinen's *Kullervo*. In 1993, Sir Peter Hall directed a new production of *The Magic Flute*, film director Herbert Ross staged a new production of *La Bohème*, and David Hockney designed Richard Strauss' *Die Frau ohne Schatten*. In January 1994, a rare staging of Manuel Penella's *El Gato Montés* with Justino Díaz, Plácido Domingo and Verónica Villarroel, was videotaped for future international broadcast. The 1994-95 season will include a Peter Sellars production of Debussy's *Pelléas et Mélisande*, new productions of *Porgy and Bess* and *Faust*, and a revival of Verdi's *Otello* with Plácido Domingo and June Anderson.

The L.A. Opera maintains a full program of community activities, including specially commissioned in-school operas, community recitals, and special performances of fully staged operas for student and underserved constituencies.

In 1997, when the new Disney Hall opens, the L.A. Opera will become the primary tenants of the Dorothy Chandler Pavilion, expecting to fill the hall for 100 performances a year. With the interest of a growing audience, the strength of a vital board of directors, and the support of the company's Founding Angels, led by Warner W. Henry, the L.A. Opera looks to the future with tremendous optimism.

PROGRAM

ENCORE!
3
TENORS

OVERTURE

From "CANDIDE"

Music by LEONARD BERNSTEIN

~

Ô SOUVERAIN! Ô JUGE! Ô PÈRE!

From "LE CID"

Music by JULES MASSENET

Text by ADOLPHE D'ENNERY, LOUIS GALLET, and EDOUARD BLAU

Performed by JOSÉ CARRERAS

~

QUANDO LE SERE AL PLACIDO

From "LUISA MILLER"

Music by GIUSEPPE VERDI

Text by SALVATORE CAMMARANO

Performed by PLÁCIDO DOMINGO

~

POURQUOI ME RÉVEILLER

From "WERTHER"

Music by JULES MASSENET

Text by EDOUARD BLAU, PAUL MILLIET

and GEORGES HARTMANN

Performed by LUCIANO PAVAROTTI

~

WITH A SONG IN MY HEART

From "SPRING IS HERE"

Music by RICHARD RODGERS Text by LORENZ HART

Performed by JOSÉ CARRERAS

~

GRANADA

Music and Spanish lyric by AGUSTÍN LARA

Performed by PLÁCIDO DOMINGO

~

NON TI SCORDAR DI ME

Music by ERNESTO DE CURTIS

Text by DOMENICO FURNÒ

Performed by LUCIANO PAVAROTTI

~

MEDLEY

A TRIBUTE TO HOLLYWOOD

Performed by JOSÉ CARRERAS, PLÁCIDO DOMINGO, and LUCIANO PAVAROTTI

~

HUNGARIAN MARCH
From "THE DAMNATION OF FAUST"
Music by HECTOR BERLIOZ

~

TU, CA NUN CHIAGNE
Music by ERNESTO DE CURTIS
Text by LIBERO BOVIO
Performed by JOSÉ CARRERAS

~

AMOR, VIDA DE MI VIDA
From "MARAVILLA"
Music by FEDERICO MORENO TORROBA
Text by ANTONIO QUINTERO and JESÚS MARIA DE AROZAMENA
Performed by PLÁCIDO DOMINGO

~

AVE MARIA
Music by FRANZ SCHUBERT
Based on a poem by SIR WALTER SCOTT
Performed by LUCIANO PAVAROTTI

~

E LUCEVAN LE STELLE
From "TOSCA"
Music by GIACOMO PUCCINI
Text by GIUSEPPE GIACOSA and LUIGI ILLICA
Performed by JOSÉ CARRERAS

~

VESTI LA GIUBBA
From "PAGLIACCI"
Music and text by RUGGIERO LEONCAVALLO
Performed by PLÁCIDO DOMINGO

~

NESSUN DORMA!
From "TURANDOT"
Music by GIACOMO PUCCINI
Text by GIUSEPPE ADAMI and RENATE SIMONI
Performed by LUCIANO PAVAROTTI

~

MEDLEY
AROUND THE WORLD
Performed by JOSÉ CARRERAS, PLÁCIDO DOMINGO, and LUCIANO PAVAROTTI

~

Ô SOUVERAIN! Ô JUGE! Ô PÈRE!

"El Cid" was Rodrigo Díaz de Vivar (in Arabic, *El Seid*—"The Conqueror"), a legendary nobleman who lived during the Moorish occupation of Spain (1043–1099 A.D.). Murder, political intrigue, and charges of treason have taken their toll and left him stripped of everything but courage. Alone and despondent in his tent on the eve of war, he laments his separation from his beloved Chimène. Far outnumbered by the opposing armies, he fears certain defeat in the coming battle. This heartfelt prayer affirms his profound faith in the Almighty, faith soon rewarded when a vision of Saint James appears to him, assuring victory.

Few details about the actual man exist. His real life, like that of most legends, seems to have been somewhat less sensational than his press. Nevertheless, tales of his reputation for courage and mercy soon found their way into the popular literature of the age. Nearly a millenium after his death, the legend of El Cid has been refreshed in our own time by the film starring America's "epic hero," Charlton Heston, with Sophia Loren as Chimène.

From "LE CID" Music by JULES MASSENET (1842–1912)
Text by ADOLPHE D'ENNERY, LOUIS GALLET,
and EDOUARD BLAU

Ah! tout est bien fini. Mon beau rêve de gloire,
Mes rêves de bonheur s'envolent à jamais!
Tu m'as pris mon amour, tu me prends
   la victoire,
Seigneur, je me soumets!
Ô souverain, ô juge, ô père,
Toujours voilé, présent toujours,
Je t'adorais au temps prospère,
Et te bénis aux sombres jours.
Je vais où ta loi me réclame,
Libre de tous regrets humains,
Ô souverain, ô juge, ô père,
Ta seule image est dans mon âme
Que je remets entre tes mains.

Ah! All is over! My dreams of glory,
My dreams of happiness have fled forever!
You have taken my love, you take my victory.
Lord, I submit myself to You!
Oh, Lord, oh, Judge, oh, Father,
You are always present in my mind.
I adored you in happy times,
And I bless You in these sorrowful days.
I go wherever You may send me,
Free of any human regrets.
Oh, Lord, oh, Judge, oh, Father,
Your image is always in my soul,
Which I place into Your hands.

QUANDO LE SERE AL PLACIDO

Love, honor and jealousy are the passions that so often propel the characters in opera. In *Luisa Miller*, Verdi arranges them in a fateful triangle, straining the loyalties of parents and children and the bonds of trust between lovers.

The story takes place in a Tyrolean village in the early eighteenth century. Luisa and Rodolfo are in love. She is the daughter of a retired soldier. He is the noble son of Count Walter, disguised as a peasant. To make matters more complicated, Luisa has agreed to marry the Count's conniving steward (whose name "Wurm" speaks volumes about his charácter). And Rodolfo has been promised by his father to a wealthy widow.

Enraged when he learns that his son loves the common Luisa, the Count imprisons her father. To save the old man's life, Luisa writes a letter to Rodolfo denying her love for him. Just as the Count and Wurm have planned, the letter falls into Rodolfo's hands. More devastated than his father could have imagined, Rodolfo resolves to kill both Luisa and himself.

Verdi's exquisite music underscores the plot as it dramatically unfolds toward its inevitable, tragic end — never more beautifully than in this aria in which Rodolfo laments his apparent betrayal.

From "LUISA MILLER"
Music by GIUSEPPE VERDI (1813 - 1901)
Text by SALVATORE CAMMARANO

Oh! fede negar potessi agl'occhi miei!
Se cielo e terra, se mortali ed angeli
attestarmi volesser ch'ella non è rea,
mentite! io responder dovrei, tutti mentite.

Son cifre sue! Tanta perfidia! Un'alma
sì nera! sì mendace!
Ben la conobbe il padre!
Ma dunque i giuri, le speranze, la gioia,
le lagrime, l'affanno?
Tutto è menzogna, tradimento, inganno!

Quando le sere al placido
chiaror d'un ciel stellato
meco figgea nell'etere
lo sguardo innamorato,
e questa mano stringermi
dalla sua man sentia...
ah! mi tradia!
Allor, ch'io muto, estatico
da'labbri suoi pendea,
ed alla in suon angelico,
"amo te sol" dicea,
tal che sembrò l'empireo
apirsi all'alma mia!
Ah! mi tradia!

Oh, if only I could deny trust in my very eyes!
If heaven and earth, if mortals and angels
were to reassure me that she is not guilty,
I should have to reply: you all lie!

This is her writing! Such treachery! A heart
so black, so false!
My father knew her well!
But what of the vows, the hopes, the joy,
the tears, the anguish?
All is falsehood, betrayal, deception!

When at eventide, in the tranquil
glimmer of a starry sky,
with me she gazed lovingly
into space
and I felt this hand of mine
pressed by hers...
Ah! She betrayed me.
Then I, silent, ecstatic,
would hang onto her words
when she in angelic tones said:
"I love you, I love only you,"
so that paradise seemed
to open to my soul!
Ah, she betrayed me!

POURQUOI ME REVELLER

It is autumn in late-19th century Frankfurt, and Charlotte has married Albert in order to keep a promise she made to her dying mother. At the wedding, she begs the young romantic dreamer, Werther, who is deeply in love with her, to leave the city rather than persist with his constant and passionate attentions. When they are reunited weeks later on Christmas eve, she knows it is Werther she truly loves in spite of her efforts to repress her feelings toward him. Together again, they are reminded of the happy memories of shared moments of beauty in their lives. Opening one of the many books they once enjoyed together, he reads to her this sad lament from the poetry of Ossian, which perfectly expresses the futility of their love.

Massenet based his opera on "The Sorrows of Young Werther," an immensely popular novel which captured the essential spirit of the Romantic Age.

From "WERTHER"
Music by JULES MASSENET (1842 – 1912)
Text by EDOUARD BLAU, PAUL MILLIET and
GEORGES HARTMANN

Pourquoi me réveiller, ô souffle du printemps?
Sur mon front je sens tes caresses,
et pourtant bien proche est le temps
des orages et des tristesses!
Pourquoi me réveiller, ô souffle du printemps?
Demain, dans le vallon, viendra le voyageur,
se souvenant de ma gloire première,
et ses yeuz vainement chercheront ma splen-
deur:
ils ne trouveront plus que deuil et que misère!
Hélas! Pourquoi me réveiller, ô souffle du
printemps?

Why awaken me, O breath of spring?
On my brow I feel thy caresses,
and yet the time of storms
and of sorrows is nigh!
Why awaken me, O breath of spring?
Tomorrow the traveller will come into the dale
recalling my former glory,
and in vain will his eyes seek my splendor:
they will find naught but mourning and
despair!
Alas! Why awaken me, O breath of spring?

WITH A SONG IN MY HEART

Mario Lanza, one of the most charismatic singers of his generation, motivated millions of fans to imitate his vocal style (if only in the shower!). He became the first "crossover" star to bridge the classical and popular repertoire, becoming RCA's top-selling recording artist in the process. Lanza's portrayal of an equally celebrated tenor in the film *The Great Caruso* (1951) inspired many of his admirers—including Mr. Carreras—to pursue serious musical careers. Lanza made a total of five films for MGM, all of them featuring remarkably popular renditions of operatic highlights.

With a Song In My Heart, one of Mario Lanza's favorites, was originally written for the Broadway show *Spring is Here* in 1929. It became a popular hit in 1952 as the title song of an inspiring biography. In the Oscar-winning film, Susan Hayward portrays Jane Froman, the popular American singer of the 30's, who makes a remarkable recovery after serious injuries sustained in a plane crash nearly ended her career.

From "SPRING IS HERE"
Music by RICHARD RODGERS (1902–1979)
Text by LORENZ HART

With a song in my heart.
I behold your adorable face,
Just a song at the start,
But it soon is a hymn to your grace.
When the music swells
I'm touching your hand;
It tells that you're standing near, and
At the sound of your voice
Heaven opens its portals to me.
Can I help but rejoice
That a song such as ours came to be?
But I always knew
I would live life through
With a song in my heart for you.

GRANADA

Granada is an exotic and magical place. Commanding the foothills of the Sierra Nevada mountains of southern Spain, it was the final stronghold of the Moors who occupied the Iberian Peninsula for seven centuries. Granada's history is enriched by its numerous contributions to art, literature and science. Its cathedral is the final resting place of Ferdinand and Isabel, the first rulers of a united Spain, who sent Columbus on his fateful journey westward.

The wondrous lore of this ancient capital is laden with tales of romance and adventure, inspired in part by the beautiful Moorish architecture and gardens of the Alhambra palace which dominate the cliffs above the city.

Granada's allure certainly inspired Mexican composer Agustín Lara, a remarkably prolific composer. He wrote more than 600 songs including "Maria Bonita" and "Solamente Una Vez."

Music and Spanish lyric by AGUSTÍN LARA (1900 - 1970)

Granada, tierra soñada por mí,
mi cantar se vuelve gitano
cuando es para ti.
Mi cantar, hecho de fantasía,
mi cantar, flor de melancolía,
que yo te vengo a dar.
Granada, tierra ensangrentada
en tardes de toros,
mujer que conserva el embrujo
de los ojos moros.
De sueño, rebelde, gitana
cubierta de flores,
y beso tu boca de grana,
jugosa manzana
que me habla de amores.
Granada, manola, cantada
en coplas preciosas,
no tengo otra cosa que darte
que un ramo de rosas,
de rosas de suave fragrancia
que le dieran marco
a la Virgen morena.
Granada, tu tierra está llena
de lindas mujeres, de sangre
y de sol.

Granada, I'm falling under your spell.
And if you could speak,
what a fascinating tale you would tell —
of an age the world has long forgotten,
of an age that weaves
a silent magic in Granada today.
The dawn in the sky greets the day
with a sigh for Granada,
For she can remember the splendor
that once was Granada.
It still can be found
in the hills all around
as I wander along,
entranced by a land
full of sunshine and flowers and song.
And soon it will welcome the stars,
while guitars play a soft habanera;
then moonlit Granada will live again
the glory of yesterday,
romantic and gay.
And when day is done
and the sun starts
to set in Granada
I envy the blush of the snowclad
Sierra Nevada.

NON TI SCORDAR DI ME

The Neapolitan song evolved during the last years of the 19th century in the sunshine of Italy's Mediterranean port city Naples, where literally thousands of melodies were written by dozens of composers. The greatest of the songwriters, including Tosti, Bixio and de Curtis, attained a perfect match of voice, artistic temperament and poetry rarely achieved in music. Their music found willing performers in the singers there, who filled the air with their evocative refrains.

Hearing them again prompts memories of long ago afternoons spent listening to these songs around the phonograph. Their lilting melodies were beloved by Gigli, di Stefano, Caruso, and many other singers whose recordings from an earlier age have become part of a lasting vocal tradition. These ballads continue to be passed along affectionately from generation to generation, and not surprisingly, each of the three tenors has recorded several albums with his own particular favorites from this repertoire.

Music by ERNESTO DE CURTIS (1863–1945)
Text by DOMENICO FURNÒ

Partirono le rondini dal mio paese freddo
  e senza sole,
Cercando primavere di viole,
Nidi d'amore e di felicità.
La mia piccola rondine partì
Senza lasciarmi un bacio,
Senza un addio partì.

Non ti scordar di me:
La vita mia legata è a te.
Io t'amo sempre più,
Nel sogno mio rimani tu.
Non ti scordar di me:
La vita mia legata è a te.
C'è sempre un nido
  nel mio cor per te.
Non ti scordar di me!

The swallows flew away from my cold
  and sunless land,
in search of spring and violets,
nests of love and happiness.
My little swallow flew away
without a kiss,
with no farewell she left.

Do not forget me:
my life is bound up in you.
I love you more and more,
my dreams are always of you.
Do not forget me:
my life is bound up in you.
There will always be a nest
  in my heart for you.
Do not forget me!

TU, CA NUN CHIAGNE

Traditionally, Neapolitan songs were performed to the music of the mandolin, guitar, or accordian, their verses sometimes going on and on to tell a complicated tale. Some are lighthearted serenades from sleepless lovers, others passionate laments by melancholy youths, but all of them are poems that capture the intimacy of friendship, the profound nature of desire, and a passionate love of nature. And above all, they are a true and intimate reflection of the Neapolitan soul.

Even though Enrico Caruso, who was born in Naples, was responsible perhaps more than anyone else for popularizing these wonderful songs, you don't have to be Neapolitan—or even Italian—to sing them. Great tenors from around Italy and the world have added to their fame. Gigli came from Ricanti in central Italy, Schipa was from Lecce in the south, di Stefano was from Sicily, and Mario Lanza was from South Philadelphia. Over the years, many of these songs have become classics, including this one, whose singer is overwhelmed with desire for an absent love.

Music by ERNESTO DE CURTIS (1863–1945)

Text by LIBERO BOVIO

Comm'è bella a muntagna stanotte…
bella accussì nun l'aggio vista maie!
'N'anema pare rassignata e stanca
sotto cuperta 'e chesta lune janca…

Tu che nun chiagne e chiagnere me faie,
tu, stanotte addò staie?
Voglio a te!
Voglio a te!
Chist' uocchie te vonno
n'ata vota vedè!

Commè calma 'a muntagna stanotte…
cchiù calma 'e mo nun l'aggio vista maie!
E tutto dorme, tutto dorme o more,
e i sulo veglio, perchè veglia Ammore…

Tu che nun chiagne e chiagnere me faie,
tu, stanotte addò staie?
Voglio a te!
Voglio a te!
Chist' uocchie te vonno
n'ata vota vedè!

How beautiful the mountain is tonight…
it has never looked this beautiful before!
It seems to be a soul, resigned and weary
beneath the candid coverlet of the moon…

You who weep not while you make me weep,
where are you tonight?
I need you!
I need you!
These eyes of mine desire
to see you once more!

How calm and quiet the mountain is tonight…
I've never seen it calm like this before!
All is asleep, all is asleep or dying,
I watch alone, for Love is watching too…

You who weep not while you make me weep,
where are you tonight?
I need you!
I need you!
These eyes of mine desire
to see you once more!

AMOR, VIDA DE MI VIDA

Zarzuela, the Spanish equivalent of Viennese operetta and Italian opera buffa, traces its roots to the 17th century. La Zarzuela, a royal hunting lodge on the outskirts of Madrid, had been converted by the 29-year-old king Philip IV into an elaborately decorated retreat. For his amusement, *fiestas de Zarzuela*, short comedies with music and singing, were devised. Spain's leading writers of the time collaborated on zarzuelas with more serious-minded subjects, but even those works maintained the popular touch; scenes with shepherds and shepherdesses singing *seguidillas* were interspersed with those of Greek gods in conversation.

While the early works bear little resemblance to the literally thousands of melodramatic and sentimental pieces which came to be popular by the turn of the last century, all zarzuelas share an intrinsically Spanish form and style. Moreno Torroba wrote more than 100 works, including the classic zarzuelas *Luisa Fernanda* and *La Chulapona*.

From "MARAVILLA"
Music by FEDERICO MORENO TORROBA (1891–1982)
Text by ANTONIO QUINTERO
and JESÚS MARIA DE AROZAMENA

Adiós, dijiste:
se va mi vida.
Llorar quisiste
por un amor que hay
que olvidar.
Te vas riendo
¡y yo me muero!
Mi dolor es saber
que no puedes llorar.

Amor, vida de mi vida,
¡qué triste es decirse adiós!
Te llevas la juventud
de éste querer sin redención,
amor que por el camino
no puedes volver atrás.
Te ríes cuando sientes
deseos de llorar.

Y pensar que te amé
con alma y vida,
y hoy te quieres
burlar de mi dolor.
Este amor que soñé
no lo puedo callar.
Fueron falsas palabras,
mentistes mil veces
tu amor, mujer.

Amor, vida de mi vida, *etc*.

¡Adiós, mi bien!
¡Ah, adiós!

You said farewell:
my life is departing.
You wished to weep
for a love
that must be forgotten.
You go, laughing,
and I am dying!
My sorrow is to know
that you cannot weep.

Love, life of my life,
how sad it is to say good-bye!
Youth deprives you
of this love, without redemption,
love that you cannot turn back
on its path.
You laugh when you feel
a wish to weep.

And to think that I loved you
with my body and soul,
and now you wish
to mock me in my grief.
I cannot suppress this love
of which I dreamed.
Your words of love
were false, woman:
you lied a thousand times.

Love, life of my life, *etc*.

Farewell, my love!
Ah, farewell!

AVE MARIA

Franz Schubert in his short life was one of history's most prolific and original composers, and one with a genius for melody. Sir Walter Scott's narrative poem, *The Lady of the Lake*, inspired this hymn to the Virgin. It is among Schubert's last and most beautiful compositions. Scott's poem includes the words of the Latin prayer, *Ave Maria*, which has been used in devotions since the 11th century. The text is based on the greeting of the angel Gabriel to Mary (St. Luke 1:28, 1:42), announcing her as the mother of Jesus. This prayer has often been set to music, but never in a lovelier way.

Gioacchino Rossini, composer of *The Barber of Seville* and many other popular operas, also found inspiration in this Scottish epic and created the opera *La Donna del Lago* from its poetic lines. Scott's other romantic ballads and novels on Scotish history provided the basis for many musical works, particularly Donizetti's opera, *Lucia di Lammermoor.*

Music by FRANZ SCHUBERT (1797–1828)

Based on a poem by SIR WALTER SCOTT (1771–1832)

Ave Maria!
Vergin del ciel,
sovrana di grazie e madre pia,
accogli ognor la fervente preghiera,
non negar a questo smarrito mio cor
tregua nel suo dolor!
Sprduta l'alma mia ricorre a te,
e piena di speme si prostra ai tuoi pié,
t'implor' e attende la bella pace
che solo tu le puoi donar.
Ave Maria!

Ave Maria!
Gratia plena,
Maria, gratia plena *etc*.
Ave, ave, Dominus tecum.
Benedicta tu in mulieribus,
et benedictus,
et benedictus fructus ventris
tui, Jesu.
Ave Maria!

Hail Mary!
Virgin of heaven,
queen of grace and holy mother,
receive a fervent prayer,
do not deny my bewildered heart
relief in its distress!
My lost soul turns to you,
and at your feet, full of hope,
implores you and awaits the sweet peace
that only you can give.
Hail Mary!

Hail Mary!
Full of grace,
Mary, full of grace *etc*.
Hail, hail, the Lord is with thee.
Blessed art thou among women,
and blessed,
blessed is the fruit of
thy womb, Jesus.
Hail Mary!

E LUCEVAN LE STELLE

It is June, 1800, and political turmoil permeates the sweltering air of the Roman summer. Bonaparte is on the march against Italy. The Roman despots have filled the detested prison of Castel Sant'Angelo with patriotic sympathizers clamoring for a Republic. The painter Mario Cavaradossi is among them, not only for aiding the cause against tyranny, but also for loving the enchanting Floria Tosca, a tempestuous and dazzlingly beautiful star of the opera. Tosca has been horrified by the lecherous advances of Baron Scarpia, the hypocritically pious chief of the Roman police. Scarpia will go to any lengths to crush the political opposition. He cruelly coerces Tosca to betray Cavaradossi, who now sits alone in his cell awaiting the dawn — and his execution.

As the faint light of morning tints the sky and the sweet song of a shepherd boy joins the tolling of distant church bells, Cavaradossi composes a final letter to his beloved. Facing death, and never more in love with life, he is overwhelmed by his memories of Tosca.

From "TOSCA"
Music by GIACOMO PUCCINI (1858 - 1924)
Text by LUIGI ILLICA and GIUSEPPE GIACOSA

E lucevan le stelle
ed olezzava la terra,

stridea l'uscio dell'orto,
e un passo sfiorava la rena...
Entrava ella, fragrante,
Mi cadea fra le braccia...
Oh, dolci baci, o languide carezze,
Mentr'io fremente
Le belle forme disciogliea dai veli!
Svan" per sempre il sogno mio d'amore...
L'ora è fuggita...
E muoio disperato!
E non ho amato mai tanto la vita!

And the stars shone
and the earth was perfumed.

The gate to the garden creaked
And a footstep rustled the sand to the path...
Fragrant, she entered
and fell into my arms...
Oh soft kisses, oh sweet abandon,
as I trembling unloosed her veils and
disclosed her beauty!
Oh vanished forever is that dream of love,
Fled is that hour...
and I desperately die.
And never before have I loved life so much!

VESTI LA GIUBBA

Canio, an actor in a troupe of strolling players, is preparing backstage for the evening's performance. Embittered by the knowledge that he has been betrayed by the woman he loves, he sings this poignant lament. It reveals the agony of a man who is paid to play the clown, but who suffers personal tragedy privately in silence. The theme is timeless, and the music perfectly captures its essence in one of the most famous songs in opera.

Opera is full of tales of gods and heroes, but hardly ever stories about the people next door. *Pagliacci* is an opera, along with *Cavalleria Rusticana*, with which it is often paired, that set a standard for the turn-of-the-century *verismo* tradition. In this style of opera, the action concerns the "realistic" true-life dramas of ordinary people and their passions. Canio is among the most taxing and emotionally draining roles in that repertoire, challenging all of the tenor's skills and resources.

From "PAGLIACCI"
Music and text by RUGGIERO LEONCAVALLO
(1858–1919)

Vesti la giubba
e la faccia infarina.
La gente paga
e rider vuole qua.
E se Arlecchin
t'invola Colombina,
ridi, Pagliaccio …
e ognun applaudirà!
Tramuta in lazzi
lo spasmo ed il pianto;
In una smorfia
il singhiozzo e'l dolore … Ah!
Ridi, Pagliaccio,
sul tuo amore infranto!
Ridi del duol
che t'avvelena il cor!

Put on your costume
and powder your face.
The audience pays
and wants to laugh.
And if Arlecchino
steals Colombina from you,
laugh, Pagliaccio …
and everyone will applaud!
Turn into jest
your anguish and sorrow,
into a grimace
your sobs and your grief …
Laugh, clown,
at your broken love,
laugh at the pain
which poisons your heart!

NESSUN DORMA!

Legendary China is the setting of this exotic fable. The beautiful and cruel princess Turandot has sworn to avenge her ancient ancestor, Princess Lou-Ling, who was murdered by an invader. Turandot promises her hand in marriage to the one who can solve her three inscrutable riddles, but death to he who fails. Although many before him have perished, a mysterious prince has fearlessly challenged Turandot and answered the questions correctly. She must now submit to his love, but the prince tells her that if she can discover his name by sunrise, he will forfeit his life. In this aria, he eagerly awaits the dawn and the victory of love, musing that no one in Peking will sleep while Turandot seeks his name, which he alone knows.

Puccini found the inspiration for this work in a fable by the eighteenth-century Venetian playwright Carlo Gozzi, fascinated by the possibilities of exploring the nature of "Turandot's amorous passion, which she has smothered so long beneath the ashes of her great pride."

From "TURANDOT"
Music by GIACOMO PUCCINI (1858–1924)
Text by GIUSEPPE ADAMI and RENATO SIMONI

Nessun dorma! Nessun dorma!
Tu pure, o Principessa,
nella tua fredda stanza
guardi le stelle che tremano
d'amore e di speranza!
Ma il mio mistero è chiuso in me,
il nome mio nessun saprà!
No, no, sulla tua bocca lo dirò,
cuando la luce splenderà!
Ed il mio bacio scioglierà
il silenzio che ti fa mia!

Dilegua, o notte!
Tramontate, stelle!
Tramontate, stelle! All'alba vincerò!
Vincerò! Vincerò!

No man shall sleep! No man shall sleep!
You too, o Princess,
in your chaste room
are watching the stars which
tremble with love and hope!
But my secret lies hidden within me,
no one shall discover my name!
Oh no, I will reveal it only on your lips,
when daylight shines forth
and my kiss shall break
the silence which makes you mine!

Depart, oh night!
Hasten your setting, you stars!
Set, you stars! At dawn I shall win!
I shall win! I shall win!

ENCORE! 3 TENORS

CREATED BY
TIBOR RUDAS

CONCERT GENERAL MANAGER
WAYNE BARUCH

ARTISTS MANAGEMENT
For Mr. Carreras – CARLOS CABALLÉ
For Mr. Domingo – NANCY SELTZER
For Mr. Pavarotti – HERBERT BRESLIN
For Mr. Mehta – GRANT GIFFORD

THE LOS ANGELES PHILHARMONIC
Managing Director
ERNEST FLEISCHMANN
President of the Board
ROBERT S. ATTIYEH

CHORUS OF THE LOS ANGELES MUSIC CENTER OPERA
General Director
PETER HEMMINGS
Chairman of the Board
BERNARD A. GREENBERG

RECORDINGS
WARNER MUSIC GROUP

COMPACT DISC, CASSETTE, VIDEO AND LASERDISC FORMATS
U.S.A. – ATLANTIC RECORDS AND A* VISION
THE ATLANTIC GROUP
WORLDWIDE – TELDEC CLASSICS INTERNATIONAL
WARNER MUSIC VISION

WORLDWIDE TELEVISION DISTRIBUTION
ALLIED ARTS INTERNATIONAL
VISION HOUSE

Rudas Theatrical Organization
President- LEE RUDAS

Executive Vice-President- IAN MACLAREN

General Manager- DICK GALLAGHER

Production Supervisor- MATTHIAS SCHREMMER

Office Manager- DAVID ELLIOTT

Assistant to Mr. Rudas- SHELBY GOERLITZ

Assistant to Mr. Rudas- TRACIE CRUZ

Comptroller- DOUG BEISWENGER

Advertising- DEAN RUDAS

Administrative Assistant- DONNA KRASNITZ

Stage Director- THOMAS REITZ

Production Manager- FRANK MILLANE

International Representatives
EUROPE- PETER RIEGER KONZERTAGENTUR GMBH

FAR EAST- LUSHINGTON ENTERTAINMENT

UNITED KINGDOM- ALLIED ENTERTAINMENT

HUNGARY- ANDRAS KÜRTHY

JAPAN- HIP PROMOTION

Legal Counsel
SCHUYLER M. MOORE FOR STROOK, STROOK AND LAVIN

JAY COOPER FOR MANATT, PHELPS & PHILLIPS

NIGEL CLAY FOR GODFREY & ALLEN

EDWIN PERLSTEIN

LOS ANGELES DODGERS, INC.
President- PETER O'MALLEY

Vice President Finance- BOB GRAZIANO

Vice President Ticketing- WALTER NASH

Vice President Stadium Operations- BOB SMITH

Vice President Marketing- BARRY STOCKHAMER

Vice President Communications- TOMMY HAWKINS

Director Ticket Operations- DEBRA DUNCAN

Director M.I.S.- MIKE MULARKY

Assistant Secretary/General Counsel- SANTIAGO FERNANDEZ

STAGE
Art Director- RENE LAGLER
Stage Scenery Design- LASZLO SZEKELY
Lighting Director- OLIN YOUNGER
Lighting Assistant- MONIQUE MILLANE

SOUND
Arena Sound Direction- JIMMY LOCK
BY SPECIAL ARRANGEMENT
WITH DECCA RECORDINGS
Sound Engineering Director- JOHN PELLOWE
BY SPECIAL ARRANGEMENT
WITH DECCA RECORDINGS
Sound Design- ALEXANDER YUILL-THORNTON II
Audio Recording Unit- REMOTE RECORDING SERVICES
Audio Post Production- CAPITOL STUDIOS

PRODUCTION SERVICES
Stage- WORLD STAGE, BROWN UNITED
Scaffolding- BROWN UNITED
Waterfall- SCENIC SERVICES,
PROP SERVICES UNLIMITED
Greens- JACKSON SHRUB SUPPLY
Terrain- FOAM-TEC INC.
Scenic Paintings- JC BACKINGS
Tents- ACADEMY TENT AND CANVAS
Host Management- RON AND ORLLYENE WALKER
Security- SPECIAL SECURITY SERVICES, GERMANY
MARTIN HOUBE, JENS KRÜGER
Insurance- ROBERTSON & TAYLOR
Public Relations- T. PATRICK, INC.,
LAISTER-DICKSON
Merchandising-
WINTERLAND
(NORTH & SOUTH AMERICA & FAR EAST)
EVENT! (U.K. & EUROPE)
PLAYBILL (AUSTRALASIA)
Charity Dinner- LEVY/PAZANTI

TELEVISION
Director- BILL COSELL
Coordinating Producer- GEOFF BENNETT
Technical Director- JOHN FIELD
TV Audio- ED GREENE
Associate Director- CHRISTINE CLARK
Video Facilities- G.C. & COMPANY

DOCUMENTARY
Executive Producer- DAVID DINKINS JR.
Directors- ROY HAMILTON, SUZANNE SMITH
Production Manager- PATTY GILLESPIE
Production Administration- KATHLEEN SHEEHAN
Technical Manager- BOB DAVIS
Associate Producers- CHUCK MCLEAN, SCOTT PARIDON
Post Production Audio- GEORGE W. MEYER
Post Production Video- DAN DAVIS, GREG MILLER
Facilities- DESERT PRODUCTION CENTER
HOWARD SCHWARTZ RECORDING

WORLD CUP USA 1994
Chairman & CEO- ALAN ROTHENBERG
Managing Director & COO- SCOTT PARKS LETELLIER
Managing Director & CAO- ELI PRIMROSE-SMITH
Executive Vice President- DOUG ARNOT
Executive Vice President- SUNIL GULATI
Executive Vice President- MARLA MESSING
Sr. Vice President/General Counsel- LEAH TUFFANELLI
Vice President Business Affairs- TONY TOLBERT
Assistant V.P. Client Services- SHANNON VUKALCIC
Manager Special Events Ticketing- TOM PACE
Special Thanks to- FÉDÉRATION INTERNATIONALE
DE FOOTBALL ASSOCIATION

SPECIAL THANKS
To our friends at Warner Music Group:
ROBERT J. MORGADO, AHMET ERTEGUN,
DOUG MORRIS, RAMON LOPEZ, PETER ANDRY,
VAL AZZOLI, TRACY NICHOLAS BLEDSOE,
JAMES CARRADINE, KAREN COLAMUSSI,
PATTE CONTE, VICKY GERMAISE,
STUART HIRSCH, PETER IKIN, MELVYN LEWINTER,
ANNE-MARIE NICOL, JORDAN ROST,
RAY STILL, and MARGARET WADE.

PROGRAM PUBLISHED BY
Collins Publishers San Francisco

PROGRAM DESIGN
Pentagram Design, San Francisco

PROGRAM TEXT BY
Samuel J. Paul

RESEARCH
Philip Caggiano

TEXT TRANSLATIONS
Direct Language Communications, Inc.

PRINTED IN THE USA BY
Hennegan, Cincinnati, Ohio

PRINTED IN EUROPE BY
Arnoldo Mondadori Editore S.p.A., Verona
Italy

PRINTED IN ASIA BY
Toppan Printing Company, Hong Kong

PHOTOGRAPHY & ILLUSTRATION CREDITS

COVER
Paul Davis

PAGE 2
Courtesy of the Rudas Organization

PAGE 3
Robert Cahen

PAGE 4-5
Henry Grossman

PAGE 6-7
Top: Richard Kee
Bottom: John Horny

PAGE 10-11
Courtesy of the Rudas Organization

PAGE 12
Robert Cahen

PAGE 13
Top right: Robert Cahen
Middle left: Winnie Klotz/Metropolitan Opera
Bottom right: © Steve J. Sherman

PAGE 14-15
Robert Cahen

PAGE 16-17
Robert Cahen

PAGE 18
Middle left: Robert Cahen
Below: Robert Cahen

PAGE 19
Top left: Robert Cahen
Middle right: Marty Sohl

PAGE 20-21
© Joe McNally/Sygma

PAGE 22-23
Vittoriano Rastelli

PAGE 24
Top right: Robert Cahen
Middle left: Robert Cahen

PAGE 25
Middle right: Robert Cahen
Bottom: © Steve J. Sherman

PAGE 26-27
Masami Hotta

PAGE 28-29
© Steve J. Sherman

PAGE 30
Top right: © Jack Vartoogian
Middle left: Courtesy of Zubin Mehta

PAGE 31
Top: Courtesy of Zubin Mehta
Bottom: © Steve J. Sherman

PAGE 32
Courtesy of Zubin Mehta

PAGE 34-35
Donald Dietz

PAGE 36-37
Ken Howard

PAGES 38 THROUGH 68:
Illustrations by Anthony Russo

LIBRETTO CREDITS

PAGE 42
Ô Souverain! Ô Juge! Ô Père!
Furnished by Sony Classical
English translation: Thomas G. Kaufman
German translation: Ingrid Trautmann

PAGE 44
Quando Le Sere Al Placido
Original text reprinted by kind permission of
Sony Classical GmbH
English translation by kind permission of
Gwyn Morris

PAGE 46
Pourqoui Me Réveiller
English translation by kind permission of
The Decca Record Company Ltd.
The original text is out copyright

PAGE 48
With a Song in My Heart
© 1929 (Renewed) Warner Bros. Inc. &
Williamson Music Company
All rights Reserved. Used by permission.

PAGE 50
Granada (Fantasía Española)
© 1932 Peer International Corporation
(CopyrightRenewed)
© 1950 Southern Music Publishing Co.
(A/Asia) Pty. Ltd.
International Copyright Secured.
Made in USA. All Rights Reserved.
Used by permission of CPP/Belwin, Inc.,
Miami, FL 33014.
Music and Spanish lyric: Agustín Lara
English translation: Dorothy Dodd

PAGE 52
Non Ti Scordar Di Me
© 1935 (Renewed) Beboton Verlag GMBH
All rights on behalf of Beboton Verlag GMBH
administered by Chappell & Co.
All Rights Reserved. Used by permission.
English translation: Avril Bardoni
German translation: Gery Bramall
French translation: Rosine Fitzgerald

PAGE 54
Tu, Ca Nun Chiagne
English translation: Avril Bardoni

PAGE 56
Amor, Vida De Mi Vida
Furnished by EMI Classics
English translation: Lionel Salter
French translation: Michael Roubinet

PAGE 58
Ave Maria
Permission granted by Decca Record
Company for translations.

PAGE 60
E Lucevan Le Stelle
Italian translation: Libretto: Illica & Giacosa
English translation furnished by EMI Classics

PAGE 62
Vesti La Giubba
Texts and English, French, and German
translations reprinted by kind permission of
Deutsche Grammophon GMBH, Hamburg
English translation: Lionel Salter
German translation: Ludwig Hartmann
French translation: Antoine Vierne.

PAGE 64
Nessun Dorma!
Permission granted by Decca Record
Company Limited for original and English
translation.
English translation: Laura Mardon

ENCORE! TENORS 3